AF290319

SAINT THOMAS AQUINAS

Reason as the Servant of Faith

Written by Mélanie Mettra
In collaboration with Damien Glad
Translated by Rebecca Neal

SAINT THOMAS AQUINAS

KEY INFORMATION

- **Born:** 1225 in the castle of Roccasecca, Kingdom of Sicily.
- **Died:** March 1274 in Fossanova Abbey, Papal States.
- **Impact:** the development of Thomism, which reconciled Catholic dogma and Aristotelian thought, and was adopted as the official doctrine of the Catholic Church.

INTRODUCTION

We tend to think of the Middle Ages as a dark period of human history, characterised by obscurantism, in contrast to the Renaissance, which saw the emergence of humanism and important scientific advances. However, this does not do the medieval era justice, as it was actually a time of considerable intellectual activity.

Thinkers from the three major monotheistic

religions (Christianity, Judaism and Islam) sought greater knowledge of God during this period, and Muslim and then Western scholars began rediscovering the philosophical writings of antiquity from the 9th century onwards. In the 12th century, European thinkers in the continent's newly founded universities participated in lively intellectual discussions, and their debates influenced theology and philosophy for centuries to come. One of the best-known of these thinkers was Thomas Aquinas, a physically imposing Doctor of the Church who taught at universities in Paris, Rome and Naples and left behind a vast body of work combining philosophy and theology. He was a prolific commentator on the Bible and the writings of Aristotle, as well as a firm believer in the importance of of and contemplation, and used his writings to show that, far from being incompatible, reason and faith are in fact two valid ways of attaining knowledge of God. He also wrote texts that paved the way for democratic and even secular thought and promoted the ideal of happiness, and his thinking plays a key role in Catholic intellectual debates even today.

BIOGRAPHY

Portrait of Thomas Aquinas.

JOINING THE DOMINICAN ORDER

Thomas Aquinas was born to a noble family in the castle of Roccasecca, near the village of Aquino from which he takes his name, in 1225. On his father's side, he was a great-nephew of Frederick I, (Holy Roman Emperor, 1122-1190). His family intended him to embark on an ecclesiastical career, so he was sent to the first Benedictine monastery at Monte Cassino to study Latin literature. During his time there, he discovered prayer and contemplation, which would be constant companions for him throughout his life and a major influence on his work. In 1240, he went to Naples to undertake more advanced studies in grammar, science, theology and above all philosophy. He also discovered the recently founded Dominican Order, which he joined as a novice after the death of his father in 1243. This displeased his mother, Theodora of Teano, who set out to look for him in Naples and then Rome in order to bring him back to the family castle and force him to pursue the career that had been chosen for him. Theodora's initial attempts to track down her son were unsuccessful, but he was eventually captured and brought home. He was kept at Roccasecca for almost a year, but refused to renounce his Dominican vows.

A LIFE DEDICATED TO TEACHING

He continued his studies in Paris after his release in 1245, and went on to study in Cologne in 1248. He was taught by Albertus Magnus (German theologian and philosopher, c. 1200-1280), one of the first theologians to base their ideas on the rediscovered works of Aristotle (Greek philosopher, 384-322 BCE). After completing his studies, Aquinas also became a teacher, initially in one of the two Dominican schools incorporated in the University of Paris. In 1259, he was recalled to Italy by Pope Alexander IV (1199-1261) and appointed theological advisor and lecturer to the papal Curia. Although he had been nicknamed "the dumb ox" by his fellow students because of his size and reserved nature, his renown and influence were by now such that Pope Urban IV (1200-1264), Alexander IV's successor, asked him to write a text challenging Aristotelian philosophy as it was taught by the Averroists at the Sorbonne.

Although Albertus Magnus is nowadays virtually unknown outside the fields of history and philosophy, it is probable that a distorted version of his name gave rise to the "Maubert" in Place Maubert, a square in Paris near the Sorbonne, which was a hub of theological education during the Middle Ages.

| Portrait of Albertus Magnus.

In 1269, Aquinas returned to the University of Paris and continued to reflect on the controversy surrounding interpretations of the works of ancient Greek philosophers, before accepting a post as the leader of a new Dominican school in Naples. In December 1273, he had a vision of his imminent death and decided to put an end to his work. Pope Gregory X (1210-1297) then summoned him to the Second Council of Lyon, which was to pronounce a judgement on the Crusades in the Holy Land and the union of the Western and Eastern Churches. He set off in January 1274, but never arrived at his destination as he fell ill on the way and died in the Cisterian abbey of Fossanova. His relics are currently housed in the Church of the Jacobins in Toulouse.

His ideas, as set out in his two masterpieces the *Summa theologiae* and the *Summa contra gentiles*, in his numerous commentaries on the Bible and the works of Aristotle, and in records of issues discussed in the course of his teaching career, were debated at length and with passion after his death. He was eventually canonised by Pope John XXII (1245-1334) on 18 July 1323 and made a Doctor of the Church in 1567.

CONTEXT

THE FOUNDING OF THE DOMINICAN ORDER

Two mendicant orders, which practised poverty and an iterant lifestyle, emerged in the 13th century. These were the Order of Friars Minor, also known as the Franciscan Order after its founder Francis of Assisi (1182-1226), and the Order of Preachers, also known as the Dominican Order, founded by the Castilian priest Dominic de Guzmán. Dominic was born in 1170 near Burgos, and studied theology and was ordained as a priest in Osma (Castile) in 1190. He was renowned for his talents as a preacher, and on two occasions he accompanied Diego de Acebo, the Bishop of Osma, to Denmark in order to help arrange the marriage between the heir to the Castilian throne and a Danish princess. Their journey took them through the south of France, where they discovered the thriving religious movement of Catharism. This provided the perfect opportunity for the young Dominic to put his ideals of preaching and evangelisation into practice.

In 1206, he founded an abbey in Prouilhe, France and gathered his first followers. He subsequently travelled around the Lauragais and the area around Carcassonne, Toulouse and Montpellier in order to convert the local inhabitants back to Catholicism from what he saw as the heresy of Catharism. He founded the Order of Preachers in 1216 with the aim of establishing a stable network of preachers, which was largely made possible by the support of Pope Innocent III (1160-1216), who saw the austerity of the new order as a good way of responding to the criticisms levelled at Catholicism by heterodox religious groups. Taking inspiration from the Roman Doctor of the Church Augustine of Hippo (354-430), the friars followed the example set by the apostles and embarked on a mission of itinerant preaching. Dominic himself travelled through France, Spain and Italy to spread the Order's message. He died in Bologna in 1221.

The Dominican Order's vocation was to preach the laws and moral teachings of Catholicism, and its ideas were based on a solid understanding of theology, canon law and philosophical doctrines.

Consequently, Dominican monasteries were primarily centres of learning and instruction. Preachers went there to learn, and returned regularly during the course of their travels for fresh ideas and inspiration. Many of its members held doctorates, and although they lived itinerant lives of poverty, the Dominicans had expert knowledge of theology, philosophy and science and were influential, insightful thinkers.

| Emblem of the Dominican Order.

THE DEVELOPMENT OF UNIVERSITIES

Throughout the Middle Ages, the Church provided education in its school and abbeys, and in

1179 Pope Alexander III (1105-1180) decreed that education should be free and scholars could teach the subjects they saw fit. In light of this increased freedom and the fact that there were more centres of learning than ever before, some scholars decided to bring students and teachers together in independent establishments dedicated to learning and instruction. These new institutions were still attached to the Church, but enjoyed their own special status. This marked the creation of the earliest European universities, such as Bologna, which specialised in law, and Salerno, which was home to the first medical guild. Philip II of France (1165-1223) gave teachers in Paris special freedoms and privileges, and granted the University of Paris its charter in 1200. The city's schools had previously been collectively known as the *studium generale*, but this name was now changed to *universitas magistrorum et scolarium parisiensium*, meaning "all the teachers and students of Paris". This is where the word "university" comes from.

THE SORBONNE

Before long, students and teachers from all over Europe began flocking to the University of Paris. They often lived in colleges, which resembled boarding houses and were a place for living and studying rather than teaching. In 1253, Robert de Sorbon (1201-1274), chaplain and confessor to King Louis X (1214/1215-1270), founded a college on Montagne Saint-Geneviève, a hill overlooking the Seine in Paris. It offered its first teaching chair in the 16th century and became the University of the Sorbonne, one of the best-known and most prestigious seats of learning in Europe.

| The Sorbonne in 1550.

The universities' main privilege was their independence from both the Church (they still came under papal authority, but no longer answered to priests or bishops) and from royal power (royal officials has no authority over university affairs, and the universities had their own security forces and courts). They also had jurisdiction over their own curriculum: they were free to research, discuss and debate the subjects they saw fit, although they regularly clashed with the authority of the pope. Most of the universities established in the 13th century, such as those of Naples (1224), Toulouse (1229) and Rome (1244), were created on the initiative of the pope.

Most of the universities' teaching was focused on four areas: canon law, theology, medicine and the arts (meaning the liberal arts, such as mathematics, philosophy, grammar and rhetoric), and most of their students went on to pursue ecclesiastical careers, although this was not necessarily the case. The members of mendicant orders, which came into existence at around the same time as the universities, were particularly well represented, as one of their key missions was to develop a Catholic doctrine and spread it through evangelism.

FROM PLATO TO ARISTOTLE

Until the 12th century, the most important influence on religious philosophy was Augustine of Hippo. Augustine came from a family of modest landowners and studied in Carthage, where he garnered recognition for his skill as a rhetorician, then in Rome. He was raised as a Christian by his mother, and briefly dabbled in Manichaeism before reconverting while teaching in Milan. He was baptised and then returned to Carthage and became Bishop of Hippo Regius, in modern-day Algeria. In his 35 years as bishop, he developed a school of doctrinal thought which combined Christianity and Neo-Platonism, studied human free will, faith and divine grace, and worked on a philosophy of knowledge which focused on intelligible truth. "Phenomena", as described by Plato (c. 427-348/347 BCE) could be uncovered by reason and knowledge, whereas Augustine, as a Christian, discussed the concept of "eternal truths" which could only be revealed by faith. This means that faith is essential for a true understanding of the world, and in Augustinian thought, faith is more important than knowledge. The free will that allows humans to choose between good and evil can only be exercised correctly with God's help. Augustine believed that our perception often deceives us, and was therefore highly sceptical of anything related to the material and physical world, largely as a result of his dissolute youth and the urges that he tried to repress. His monumental body of work laid the foundations of Catholic doctrine, and to this day the Church's teachings are influenced by his thought.

| Portrait of Augustine of Hippo by Philippe de Champaigne.

From the 9th and 10th centuries onwards, the brilliant work of Arab scholars revolutionised philosophy, and by extension Western theology.

The scientific revolution that was sweeping through the Islamic world was accompanied by the large-scale translation of ancient Greek authors, whose work combined science and philosophy. In the 9th century, Baghdad became the hub of this new movement, and texts by Ptolemy (Greek scholar, c. 100-c. 170), Galen (Greek doctor, c. 131-c. 201) and Aristotle were retranslated. In the 12th century, Arabic translations, and above all the commentaries that accompanied them, in particular those by Avicenna (Iranian philosopher and doctor, 980-1037), Averroes (Muslim philosopher, 1126-1198) and Maimonides (Jewish theologian, philosopher and doctor, 1138-1204), which had in turn been translated into Latin, circulated throughout Europe. Aristotle's texts, particularly his *Physics* and *Metaphysics*, were met with unprecedented enthusiasm, although the papal authorities were decidedly less convinced, and initially banned them. Indeed, the main subject of the passionate debates between 13th-century thinkers, including Thomas Aquinas, was Aristotelian philosophy and its myriad interpretations.

KEY MOMENTS

ARISTOTELIAN THOUGHT AND THE CONTROVERSY OVER LATIN AVERROISM

While some previously undiscovered works by Aristotle circulated in the Islamic world as early as the 11th century, the papal authorities did not authorise Western universities to read and study them until the 13th century. Specifically, Pope Gregory IX (c. 1170-1241) gave his authorisation for the *Physics* and *Metaphysics*, as well as Latin translations of a number of Arabic, Persian, Jewish and Greek works, to be included on university syllabuses in 1231 (it is worth mentioning that, prior to this, many teachers had taught these works secretly in spite of the official ban). By 1250, all of Aristotle's works were well-known in the Western world, and at around this time they began to feature on examinations in the Faculty of Arts at the University of Paris, which gave rise to a multitude of differing interpretations.

In 1265, Siger of Brabant (1235-1281/1284), a member of the Faculty of Arts, developed a new school of thought, which he claimed was inspired by Averroes's criticisms of works of Greek philosophy. For this reason, it became known as Latin Averroism, although it was not entirely consistent with Averroist philosophy. One of Siger and his followers' main ideas was that philosophy and revelation are independent from one another: revelation cannot be attained through philosophy, and truth can be accessed through philosophy alone without being ac-companied by revelation. Underlying this belief is the idea that God is not directly behind every event. Another of Latin Averroism's key theories posits the existence of an active intellect, which could be God himself, outside the human soul. This means that there is a soul that is shared by all humans rather than being distinct for each person, and an external intellect that allows them to understand and pass judgement on the world. Finally, Siger shared Aristotle's belief that the world is eternal, with no beginning or end.

These three ideas sparked outcry within the Church, as they challenged a number of its doctrines. Specifically, according to the Bible, the world has a beginning, humans have free will and each person has a distinct soul. Furthermore, the Church rejected the claim that philosophy alone could lead to the truth, as there was a possibility that it could use sophistry to apparently prove that God does not exist, in which case it would necessarily be false and deceptive. Consequently, in 1268 Gilles de Lessines (died in 1304) asked Albertus Magnus to produce a written refutation of the theories of the Latin Averroists, and in 1270 the Bishop of Paris outlawed their teachings.

During the same period, another Western philosopher, Boetius of Dacia (died c. 1284), drew inspiration from Aristotle's works and Averroes's commentaries to try and reconcile the Aristotelian belief in the eternity of the world and the Bible's assertion that it has a beginning, while also denying humankind's free will. However, Albertus Magnus was the first true Aristotelian philosopher of this period, and worked to reconcile Aristotelian thought and Catholic theology. He followed Aristotle's example by affirming that philosophy should focus on studying natural phenomena and their natural causes, using an approach that resembles that of the natural sciences, without assuming that these phenomena stem from divine will or divine intentions, but rather seeing them as a manifestation of divine will.

Aquinas studied under Albertus Magnus and returned to Paris in 1269 as a teacher. He went on pursue his former teacher's work to reconcile philosophy and theology.

AQUINAS AND SCHOLASTICISM

Aquinas is widely regarded as one of the most important Scholastic thinkers. Scholasticism sought to reconcile faith (which implies revelation) and reason (which implies the use of the intellect), and gave rise to a new way of studying biblical texts. This approach involved reading a given text and dividing it into smaller parts in order to wring the exact meaning out of every word and turn of phrase, and in doing so precisely identify all the text's themes. An impeccable knowledge of grammar and stylistics were therefore necessary in order to flawlessly interpret the text's literal meaning. Once each part had been isolated, it was subject to *questii* ("questions"), which is where philosophy came in: the scholar's aim here was to identify the deeper meaning and theological significance of the text. Finally, all the questions could be grouped together and commented on by other theologians.

This method was challenged from the 14th century onwards, particularly with the emergence of humanism. Humanists criticised the Scholastics for studying second- or third-hand rather than original texts, and for merely speculating rather than putting their ideas to the test. In spite of these criticisms, Scholasticism remained the preferred method of exegesis within the Catholic Church.

AQUINAS'S MASTERPIECES

Aquinas's output was so prolific that it is difficult to quantify. He was a tireless worker (intellectual exhaustion was almost certainly a contributing factor in his early death) who wrote texts commissioned by others and some liturgical works, but most of his writing was linked to his teaching. For example, he produced collections of the questions debated at the University of Paris, commentaries on the Bible and on Aristotle's 13 known works, and three famous works which laid out the key principles of Thomist thought.

The first of these was a collection of commentaries on *The Four Books of Sentences* by the theologian Peter Lombard (c. 1100-1160). This mid-12th century work featured biblical texts accompanied by commentaries by the Church Fathers for the purpose of illustrating the similarities and contradictions between them, which would in turn allow the Scholastic method to be applied, as was typical of university teaching. In the 13th century, it was a key reference work for professors and students at faculties of arts across the Western world, and Aquinas drew a great deal of inspiration from it when developing his own teaching methods.

THE CHURCH FATHERS

The Church Fathers were the Christian thinkers and authors whose lives and works contributed to the development of Christian doctrine in the early days of the Church (1st-8th centuries). In total, there were around 70 Church Fathers, and unlike the Doctors of the Church, they were not chosen by the papal authorities (although many Church Fathers were also Doctors of the Church). The best-known Church Fathers include Tertullian (155-222), Origen of Alexandria (185-252/254), Basil of Caesarea (330-379), Gregory of Nyssa (335-394), Saint Ambrose (340-397), Augustine of Hippo and Pseudo-Dionysius the Areopagite (late 5th-early 6th century). The Church Fathers were recognised by the Church for their contribution to theology and recorded on an official retrospective list from 1295 onwards (the year that the title Doctor of Theology was created). As new contemporary thinkers or older Fathers gained recognition for their work, their names were added to the list.

Between 1258 and 1265, Aquinas wrote the *Summa contra gentiles*. In line with the Dominican Order's mission to preach the true Christian message, this text outlined ways of persuading nonbelievers (particularly Muslims) and converting them to Christianity.

Finally, from 1266 onwards, he wrote the *Summa theologiae*, although he died before completing it. This work is divided into three parts: the first focuses on God and the knowledge of God, the second sets out guidelines for a moral life, and the third studies the life of Christ and the lessons that can be drawn from it.

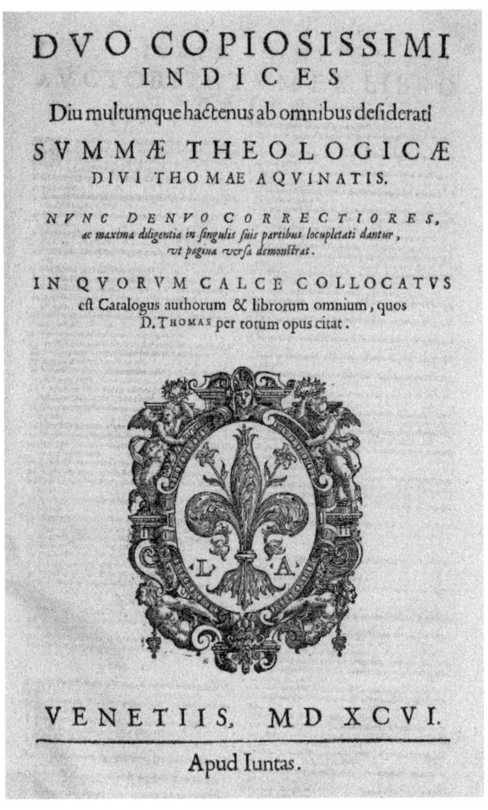

Aquinas's *Summa theologiae*.

All of Aquinas's work is based on a constant dialogue between him and earlier authors who worked on the texts he studied. He sometimes went through Averroes or Maimonides's commentaries on Aristotle's *Metaphysics* point by point in order to add his own views, express his agreement or add nuance. Thomist thought therefore synthesises the ideas of the Christian authors studied by Lombard, such as Augustine of Hippo and Pseudo-Dionysius the Areopagite, the Jewish thought of Maimonides and the Muslim theology of Averroes to create an original form of ecumenism.

REACHING GOD THROUGH REASON

Unlike Averroes and his Latin followers, Aquinas did not believe that philosophy and theology were independent, but considered them to be closely linked. Although he described philosophy as the "handmaid of theology", this does not mean that he thought it was of secondary importance: theology could not develop without the support of philosophy, so the two disciplines were interdependent. For him, humankind's ultimate goal is to achieve perfect knowledge of the perfect object in the most perfect way possible; in other words, to attain intellectual knowledge of God. However, we cannot achieve this goal ourselves as, contrary to the claims of

Augustinian thinkers and Franciscan theologians, we do not have the necessary intuition. For Aquinas, philosophy is the most important factor in understanding the ultimate purpose of human life, and reason and intellect are essential elements in the development of theology and knowledge of God. The Bible, which is the word of God and therefore a way of knowing Him, is not immediately accessible. In order to understand the divine essence it contains, we must develop our intellect, learn, try to understand all possible interpretations, and debate with a range of different readers and commentators. Similarly, nature and the world around us are proof of the divine essence. We can therefore prove the existence of God by experiencing and understanding nature, then by rationally analysing the information it provides us with. However, while philosophy can lead to an initial encounter with the divine essence, complete divine knowledge is only possible through revelation.

Reason therefore complements faith, and vice versa: reason and intellect serve faith by allowing us to attain knowledge of God's existence, but this knowledge cannot be fully acquired without faith. Similarly, philosophy and theology also complement one another: by studying the manifestations of God, philosophy (and science) can prove that He exists, while theology carries the promise of knowledge of the divine essence after death. Aquinas's work therefore combined the information that could be grasped through reason and the true knowledge that could be attained through faith.

Aquinas argued that the exercise of reason, not just its results, was a way of knowing God. In his view, the ability to think is a sort of divine spark that has been placed in each of us, and the Holy Spirit uses our intellect to guide us towards the truth. Human reason is therefore a reflection of divine intelligence. All humans are created in God's image, and when we think, we join with Him.

Critical philosophy was also a way of dealing with one of the key concerns of the time, which the first leader of the Dominican Order was particularly preoccupied by, namely the allegedly heretical beliefs that proliferated in the 13th century. The Dominicans were staunchly opposed to any form of religion based on superstition, and saw knowledge and reason as the best weapon against this scourge.

A NEW CONCEPTION OF THE SOUL

Unlike Aristotle, Averroes and Maimonides, who all saw the intellect as separate from the human soul, Aquinas viewed the intellect as part of the soul, as for him it was individual, personal and immortal. Each person has their own way of thinking, understanding and interpreting the world, which means that their thoughts cannot be governed by an external intellect. We each have our own soul, and make free use of it.

According to Aquinas, the souls of all living creatures comprise two parts: the vegetative soul, which governs growth, nutrition and reproduction, and the sensitive soul, which controls movement and feelings. Human souls have two additional functions: a cogitative power, which allows us to process the information provided by our senses, and reminiscence, which allows us to form mental images in our memory. Both of these functions rely on our intelligence, and together constitute our passive intellect. Humans also differ from animals in that they are the only living creatures to possess a rational soul. This enables abstract thought thanks to the exercise of reason, which is a function of an active intellect. This original philosophical approach to the mind was ahead of its time, and even has some similarities to concepts in modern-day neuroscience.

As well as believing that each person had their own soul, Aquinas thought that we possess free will, which allows us to choose whether or not to comply with God's wishes. Aquinas's conception of freedom is complex, because it recognises both that we have free will and that our actions can be guided by divine intervention. His reflections on free will also took on a political dimension, as he believed that humans were free to accept or reject social rules. Like Aristotle before him, Aquinas's reflections encompassed all aspects of humanity, because God was seen as the architect of every aspect of humanity, meaning that we cannot know Him perfectly without appreciating all parts of His creation.

AN ORIGINAL POLITICAL OUTLOOK

Given that humans are free to act in accordance with their own inclinations, society's wellbeing relies on moral standards supported by laws designed to protect the common good. It followed that a higher authority would be necessary to enforce these laws. Although the Catholic Church was God's representative on earth, and consequently the highest authority in matters of faith, Aquinas did not recognise its authority in temporal matters. Instead, he advocated personal authority – he was living in a medieval society in which power was vested in the sovereign, king or emperor – but insisted that it had to be representative of the people. In concrete terms, the people should be able to participate in their own government by selecting their representatives within a monarchy or oligarchy, meaning that Aquinas's political thought amounted to an early democratic system.

THE MORALITY OF HAPPINESS

In addition to political morality, Aquinas also set out a new personal morality. This was not based on laws dictated by the Church, as blindly following rules is antithetical to the exercise of reason, which is the foundation of free will and the enlightened distinction between good and evil. Instead, Aquinas followed Aristotle's example and put forward a moral system based on happiness. For him, happiness is the realisation of good, and for humans this can be achieved by satisfying our desire to know and understand. Unlike Augustine of Hippo, Aristotle and Aquinas therefore believed that happiness could be attained on earth, not just after death. However, the two thinkers differed in that, while Aristotle thought that the satisfaction of our desires was enough to make us happy, Aquinas believed that there could be no perfect happiness without knowledge of the divine.

AQUINAS'S DEATH

On 6 December 1273, when Aquinas was attending a mass for Saint Nicholas in the chapel of the same name in Naples, he had a mystical experience. Some have interpreted this as a divine vision, while others suggest it was more likely to have been a stroke. Whatever the truth, the experience wrought a drastic change in the theologian: he claimed to have seen Jesus, who congratulated him on his work and asked what would complete it, to which he responded simply "you". After this vision, he abandoned all his writing, leaving the *Summa theologiae* unfinished. When asked why he had stopped working, he responded that he had understood the insignificance of his labours, which were "like straw" compared with the momentous truths that had been revealed to him.

He went to stay with his sister to recuperate, but his condition continued to deteriorate sharply and he was left virtually mute. His brother was worried about his seemingly vacant gaze and encouraged him to go back to writing, but Aquinas told him that the time for writing was past and that he was waiting for death to attain what had been revealed to him on 6 December. Pope Gregory X then summoned him to Lyon, and on the way there he stopped at Fossanova Abbey. He then reportedly began writing a commentary on the Song of Songs: the theme of love for God, Jesus and his fellow human beings therefore remained a constant feature of his work even in his final days.

IMPACT

CONTROVERSIAL IDEAS

During Aquinas's lifetime and for several decades after his death, his ideas sparked controversy and heated debate, not only among his critics, but also among his fellow Dominicans.

In 1270, the bishop of Paris, Étienne Tempier (died in 1279) condemned 13 propositions put forward by commentators on Aristotle. In 1277, this condemnation was extended to 219 propositions, whose subjects included miracles, direct or indirect causality by God (in other words, does God intervene directly in earthly phenomena, or is this intervention carried out by intermediaries?) and the eternal existence of the world. While the condemnation primarily targeted Averroists, particularly Siger of Brabant, it was aimed more broadly at Aristotelianism and anyone who had studied and taught it, such as Aquinas. Tempier and the college of theologians he convened to study the questions debated at the Faculty of Arts in Paris were believers in authentic

Augustinianism, and Aristotelianism stood in opposition to this belief. Aquinas's stance on the unity of the soul and the body, and his belief that the body (and the senses) contributed to the work of the soul – and, by extension, that the materiality of nature is inextricably linked to divine essence – clashed with Augustine's rejection of the material world. Aquinas's fellow Dominican Robert Kilwardby (1215-1279), the Archbishop of Canterbury, also condemned his belief that mind and matter were one. However, this vehement criticism was confined to a small number of opponents, and Tempier's successor was quick to annul the 1277 condemnation. Meanwhile, the University of Paris continued to teach Averrroist ideas, Thomism and Aristotelian philosophy.

Nonetheless, the conflict between Dominicans and Franciscans continued to intensify, and the theological sparring between them did not abate until several decades later. Leading Franciscan theologians, including Saint Bonaventure (1217/1221-1274) and his followers, who also had close links with Augustinianism, Duns Scotus (1266-1308) and William of Ockham (c. 1285-c. 1349), challenged the idea that reason is an independent faculty and can allow us to access the truth, claiming instead that reason amounts to nothing without divine intervention.

| Stained glass window depicting William of Ockham in a church in Surrey.

William of Ockham, a leading figure in the philosophical school of nominalism, rejected Plato's theory of universals and fiercely opposed Aquinas's ideas about the power of reason, although his approach shared some similarities with Aristotelianism, as it was based on logic and the experience of concrete facts. In his view, reason could not lead to knowledge of God, because it was only able to grasp the information transmitted by perception. However, Aquinas's canonisation in 1323 put an end to these philosophical and theological debates.

UNIVERSALS

In Platonic philosophy, "universals", which could be referred to more simply as "ideas" or verbally expressed "thoughts", are related to language, expression and the representations of objects. According to realists (including Plato, Aristotle, and Aquinas in the Middle Ages), perception is relative: an object or thing is never identical, whereas the idea of it is fixed. For example, the idea of a tree is universal, but each individual tree is different. Universal knowledge of the tree, and the act of writing "tree", precedes the experience of the uniqueness of the tree, in the same way that the thing exists even if our senses have not experienced it directly. This means that the universe has meaning in and of itself, and this meaning is discovered by humans rather than being conferred by them.

For nominalists like William of Ockham, our ideas of a thing follow on from our experience of it. A concept (such as a tree) cannot be named until we have experienced it. Without experience, "tree" is just a word, a sound that does not carry any particular meaning.

Finally, for conceptualists, such as the French philosopher and theologian Peter Abélard (1079-1142), words do not necessarily apply to real things: we can construct concepts that have no counterpart in reality, but that are brought to life by language.

THE LEGACY OF THOMISM

The 24 Thomistic Theses and the Five Ways

The 24 Thomistic Theses are 24 sentences which sum up certain elements of Aquinas's thought on the soul and matter, will and intellect, and the existence of God. They are complemented by the Five Ways, which allow believers to prove the existence of God and know God through reason:

- **The argument from motion.** Since all motion can only come from a previous motion, the first motion can only come from an initial motion caused by God.
- **The argument from causation.** Just as all motion depends on an initial motion, all events have a cause and effect. There must therefore be an initial cause, and this can only be God.
- **The argument from contingency.** For something to exist, it must have been brought into being by something that existed before it. The first thing to exist can only be God.
- **The argument from degree.** Everything

in nature has a certain inherent degree of perfection, but for this kind of scale to make sense there must be a reference point. This reference point is God, who represents absolute perfection.

- **The argument from design.** Every living thing, each part of every living thing, and every element of nature has a purpose and a function. This purpose has been determined by an intelligent being: God.

Aquinas's canonisation was first requested by the Dominican province of Sicily in 1317, and was supported by Pope John XXII, who confirmed it in Avignon in 1323. This essentially wiped the slate clean of earlier criticism, and Thomist thought began to be taught in universities again. However, Aquinas's renown and the spread of his works are largely due to the German reformer and theologian Martin Luther (1483-1546). In response to the threat posed by the Reformation, Pope Paul III (1468-1549) convened the Council of Trent, which met for the first time in December 1545, and continued to meet regularly over the next 18 years. This Council aimed to clarify, develop and strengthen Catholic doctrine, which

Aquinas's work was an important part of.

Aquinas was named a Doctor of the Church in 1567, and before long his *Summa theologiae* superseded Peter Lombard's *Sentences* in universities. Catholic reformers, including the recently founded Society of Jesus (better known as the Jesuits), led by the Spanish Catholic priest Ignatius of Loyola (1491-1556), also drew on his arguments in their disputes with Protestant reformers.

In 1897, Pope Leon XIII (1810-1903) reaffirmed Aquinas's place in Catholic theological teaching, firstly with the encyclical (a letter sent by the Pope to bishops around the world) *Aeterni Patris*, in which he asked Christian philosophers and theologians to develop a doctrine based on Thomism, and then with his support for the creation of a commission for the study of Aquinas's works in 1879. The members of this commission were tasked with rereading his manuscripts and publishing versions that were as faithful as possible to the originals. It is still active today, and is currently managed by the Dominican Order.

At the start of the 20th century, the Catholic

Church found itself facing another doctrinal crisis due to the emergence of modernism, which advocated relativism and greater perspective with regard to Catholic texts and doctrines. In response, Pope Pius X (1835-1914) declared Scholastic philosophy and the 24 Thomistic Theses to be the fundamental components of theological teaching. In 1950, Pope Pius XII (1876-1956) reaffirmed the importance of Thomist philosophy within Catholicism in the encyclical *Humani Generis.* After some more uncertain periods, the Second Vatican Council (1962-1965) and the popes John Paul II (1920-2005) and Benedict XVI (born in 1927) confirmed Aquinas's central position in Catholic doctrine.

IN CONCLUSION

This brief introduction to Aquinas's vast body of work has focused on his philosophy, but his thought spanned many more domains, including illumination, grace, man as the image of God, angels, the Gospels and the importance of love. Indeed, the scope and importance of Aquinas's work is far too great to be covered in a single volume.

SUMMARY

- In the 12th century, Arabic translations of ancient Greek philosophers, including Aristotle, arrived in Europe, radically transforming philosophical and theological thought on the continent, which had previously been based on the writings of Plato and Neo-Platonists such of Augustine of Hippo.
- The first universities and the mendicant orders, including the Dominican Order founded by Dominic de Guzmán, appeared in the first half of the 13th century.
- Thomas Aquinas was born in the castle of Roccasecca in 1225.
- After studying at the Benedictine monastery at Monte Cassino, the young Aquinas entered the Dominican Order, to his family's dismay. Their opposition was such that his mother had him seized while he was travelling and brought back to the family castle.
- After a year at home, which did nothing to lessen his desire to be a part of the Dominican Order, Aquinas continued his studies in Paris

and then Cologne. He was taught by Albertus Magnus, who introduced him to Aristotelian philosophy.

- After becoming a doctor of philosophy, he developed a philosophy that combined Christianity and Aristotelianism and faith and reason, in opposition to the Latin Averroists, namely Siger of Brabant and his followers.
- Although his ideas were initially highly controversial, Aquinas was canonised by Pope John XXII on 18 July 1323 and made a Doctor of the Church in 1567.
- In 1914, Pope Pius X placed the 24 Thomistic Theses and the Five Ways at the heart of Catholic theological teaching.
- A series of 19th- and 20th-century popes, including John Paul II and Benedict XVI, have reaffirmed the importance of Aquinas's work in Catholic theology.

We want to hear from you!
Leave a comment on your online library
and share your favourite books on social media!

FURTHER READING

BIBLIOGRAPHY

- Attali, J. (2004) *Raison et foi : Averroès, Maïmonide, Thomas d'Aquin.* Paris: Éditions de la Bibliothèque nationale de France.

- Burlot, J. (1990) *La civilisation islamique.* Paris: Hachette.

- Chelini, J. (1991) *Histoire religieuse de l'Occident médiéval.* Paris: Hachette.

- Humbrecht, T-D. (2006) *Théologie négative et noms divins chez saint Thomas d'Aquin.* Paris: Vrin.

- Imach, R. and Oliva, A. (2009) *La philosophie de Thomas d'Aquin.* Paris: Vrin.

- Lancel, S. (No date) Augustin (saint). *Encyclopédie berbère.* [Online]. [Accessed 10 October 2014]. Available from: <http://encyclopedieberbere. revues.org/1222>

- Le Goff, J. (2012) *Hommes et femmes du Moyen Âge.* Paris: Flammarion.

- Piché, D. (1999) *La condamnation parisienne de 1277.* Paris: Vrin.

- Pouliot F. (2005) *La doctrine du miracle chez Thomas d'Aquin.* Paris: Vrin.

ADDITIONAL SOURCES

- Lindsay, J. (1904) The Philosophy of Aquinas. *Bibliotheca Sacra.* [Online]. [Accessed 25 January 2018]. Available from: <http://www.galaxie.com/article/bsac061-243-04>

NOVELS

- Alighieri, D. (2012) *The Divine Comedy: Inferno, Purgatorio, Paradiso.* Trans. Kirkpatrick, R. London: Penguin.

- Eco, U. (2004) *The Name of the Rose.* London: Vintage.

ICONOGRAPHY

- *The Virgin and Child with Saints Dominic and Thomas Aquinas*, fresco by Fra Angelico (Italian painter, 1400-1455), c. 1440, housed at the Hermitage in St. Petersburg.

- *Saint Thomas Aquinas with the* Summa, painting by Fra Angelico, c. 1442, housed at the Museo Nazionale de San Marco in Florence.

- The Demidoff Altarpiece, polyptych by Carlo Crivelli (Italian painter, c. 1430/1435-c. 1493-1500), 1476, housed at the National Gallery in London.

- *Triumph of Saint Thomas Aquinas*, painting by

Gozzoli Benozzo (Italian painter, 1420-1497), 1484, housed at the Louvre in Paris.

ICONOGRAPHIC SOURCES

- Portrait of Thomas Aquinas. Royalty-free reproduction picture.

- Portrait of Albertus Magnus. Royalty-free reproduction picture.

- Emblem of the Dominican Order. Royalty-free reproduction picture.

- The Sorbonne in 1550. Royalty-free reproduction picture.

- Portrait of Augustine of Hippo by Philippe de Champaigne. Royalty-free reproduction picture.

- Aquinas's *Summa theologiae*. Royalty-free reproduction picture.

- Portrait of William of Ockham. Royalty-free reproduction picture.

Although the editor makes every effort to verify the accuracy of the information published, 50Minutes. com accepts no responsibility for the content of this book.

www.50minutes.com

Ebook EAN: 9782808002622

Paperback EAN: 9782808008310

Legal Deposit: D/2018/12603/50

Cover: © Primento

Digital conception by Primento, the digital partner of publishers.